Braille

for the

Sighted

Designed and illustrated by
Jane Schneider and Kathy Kifer

Published by
Garlic Press
605 Powers Street
Eugene, OR 97402

www.garlicpress.com
Printed in China

ISBN 0-931993-95-4
Reorder Number GP-095

Introduction

Have you ever wondered how braille dots are organized so that people can read them with their fingers? Would you like to read braille as a sighted person? If braille is an interest to you, you will enjoy what is to follow.

Background 4
A - J Recognition 6
K - T Recognition 8
U - Z Recognition 10
Alphabet Answers 12
Hidden Pictures 14
Matching 16
Find the Mismatch 17
Analogies 18
Compound Words 19
Capital Letters 20
Answering Questions 21
Sounds Good to Me 22
Wordsearch 23
Crossword Puzzle 24
Numbers 25
Number Practice 26
Answers 28

Braille is a system of communication for those who are blind or who have severe vision difficulties. It is a system of raised dots which represent letters and numbers.

Braille takes its name from its creator, Louis Braille. Louis, born in France in 1809, lost his sight at age three, the result of an accident. Louis was a bright and eager learner. At the age of fifteen, he had completed an alphabet consisting of raised dots in groups of six combined with short dashes.

Louis adapted and perfected his system of raised dots. He wrote a book at age twenty, explaining his reading and writing methods that would become known worldwide as braille.

A slate and stylus are frequently used today by blind people for writing. A slate is made of two metal or plastic pieces hinged together. A piece of heavy paper is placed between the two hinged pieces. The top of the slate has window-like openings, each the same size as a braille cell.

A stylus is a pointed tool used to punch raised dots onto paper. The stylus is moved from cell to cell, making raised letters to spell out written words. A braille "eraser" has a blunt tip to press a dot flat.

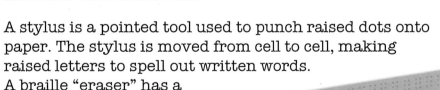

Eraser

Slate

Stylus

A braille writer using a slate and stylus must write from right to left, brailling letters backwards. The raised dots are formed on the back of the paper. The dots face upwards when the paper is turned over.

A slate and stylus are used by blind people as sighted people use a pad and pencil. A brailler also exists. It is like a typewriter that punches out braille cells. Computer systems which have regular keyboards can translate to special printers to produce raised braille cells.

The braille alphabet is formed within a braille cell. A braille cell is a group of six dots. Braille letters are made by raising one or more dots in the cell.

The six dot positions within the cell are numbered and referred to as dot 1, dot 2, dot 3, dot 4, dot 5, and dot 6.

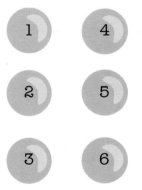

Because this book does not use raised dots, raised dots will be shown as large dots. The small dots do not show in actual braille.

The following lessons and activities will teach you the very basics of braille. Finer points of braille grammar and spelling will be left for another time. Ready?

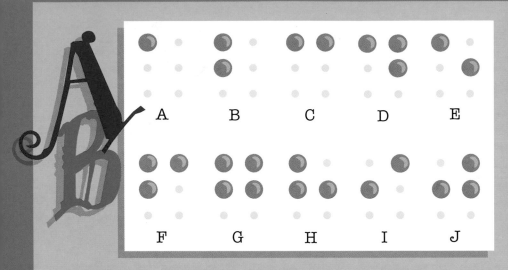

Note how the letters A-J are made in the upper two-thirds of the cell. Can you identify these words?

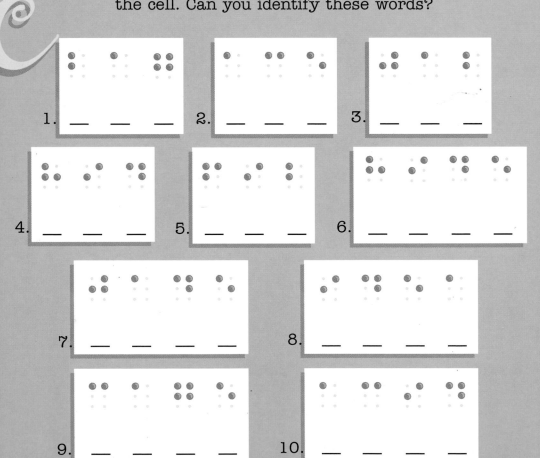

1. __ __ __

2. __ __ __

3. __ __ __

4. __ __

5. __ __ __

6. __ __ __ __

7. __ __ __ __

8. __ __ __ __ __

9. __ __ __ __

10. __ __ __ __

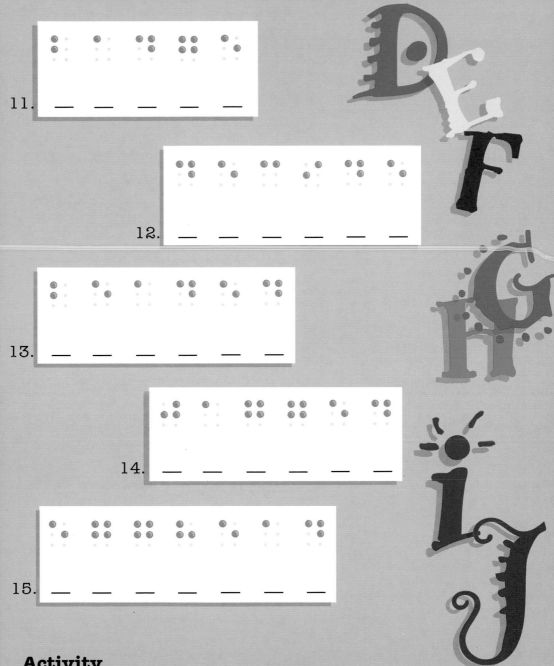

11. __ __ __ __ __

12. __ __ __ __ __ __

13. __ __ __ __ __ __

14. __ __ __ __ __ __

15. __ __ __ __ __ __ __

Activity

Begin making a set of braille alphabet flash cards with braille on one side and the regular alphabet on the other. Begin with A-J. Add the remaining letters of the alphabet as they are introduced.

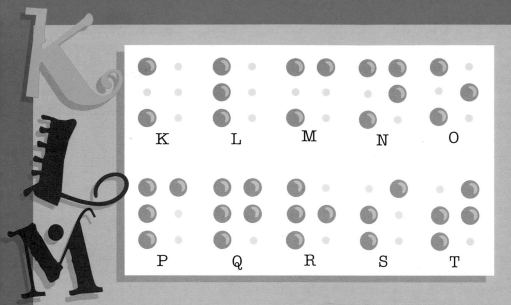

K L M N O

P Q R S T

Note how the letters K - T are formed by adding dot 3 to A - J.

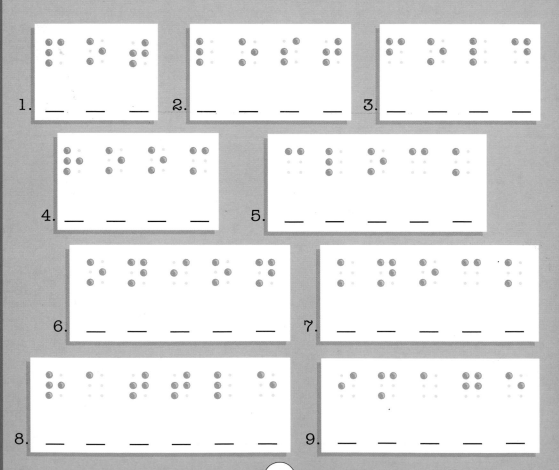

1. ___ ___ ___

2. ___ ___ ___

3. ___ ___ ___

4. ___ ___ ___

5. ___ ___ ___ ___

6. ___ ___ ___ ___

7. ___ ___ ___ ___

8. ___ ___ ___ ___

9. ___ ___ ___

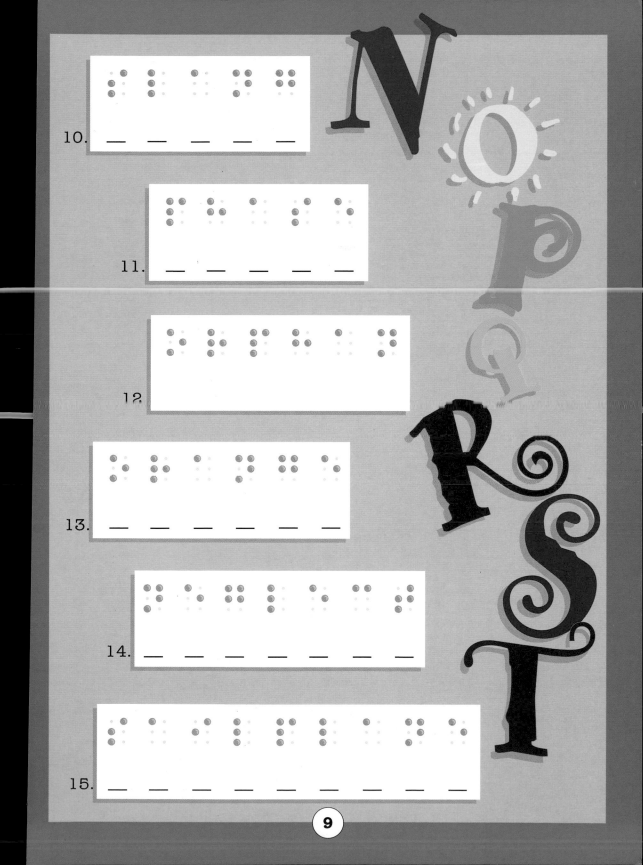

10. __ __ __ __ __

11. __ __ __ __ __

12. __ __ __ __ __ __

13. __ __ __ __ __ __

14. __ __ __ __ __ __

15. __ __ __ __ __ __ __

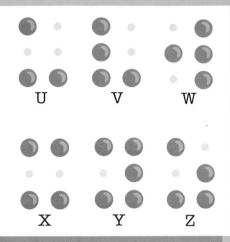

U   V   W

X   Y   Z

Add dot 6 to K, L, *J*, M, N, O.
(*J* is out of order. The "rule" doesn't work.)

1. __ __ __   2. __ __ __

3. __ __ __   4. __ __ __   5. __ __ __

6. __ __ __   7. __ __ __

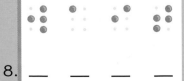 

8. __ __ __ __   9. __ __ __ __ __

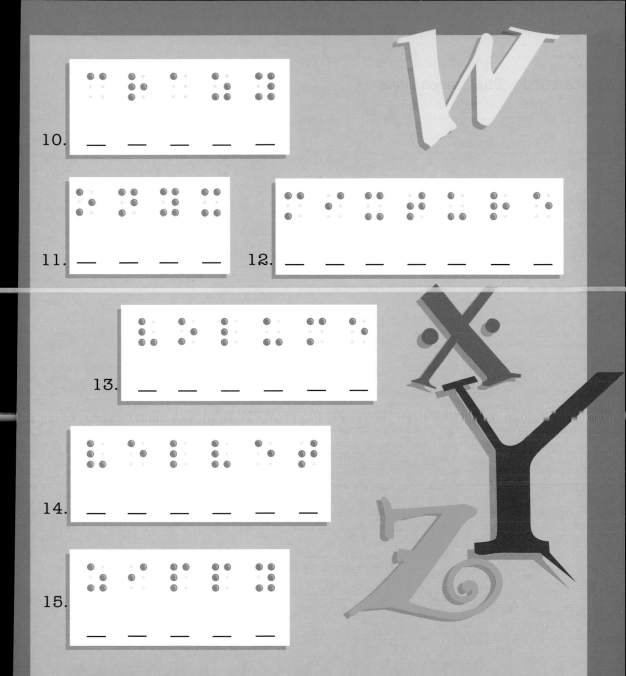

10. __ __ __ __

11. __ __ __ __   12. __ __ __ __ __ __ __

13. __ __ __ __ __ __

14. __ __ __ __ __ __

15. __ __ __ __ __

Activity

Two players. You should have 26 flash cards now. Place the cards, with the braille side down, in a stack. Alternate turning top card over. First one to correctly identify the card keeps the card. If the card is not identified after one guess by each player, the next card is flipped.

Alphabet Answers

Which alphabet letters answer these descriptions?

1. A blue bird (⠿) ____

2. A drink (⠿) ____

3. Spanish for yes (⠿) ____

4. Something you see with (⠿) ____

5. Expression of surprise (⠿) ____

6. Another expression of surprise (⠿) ____

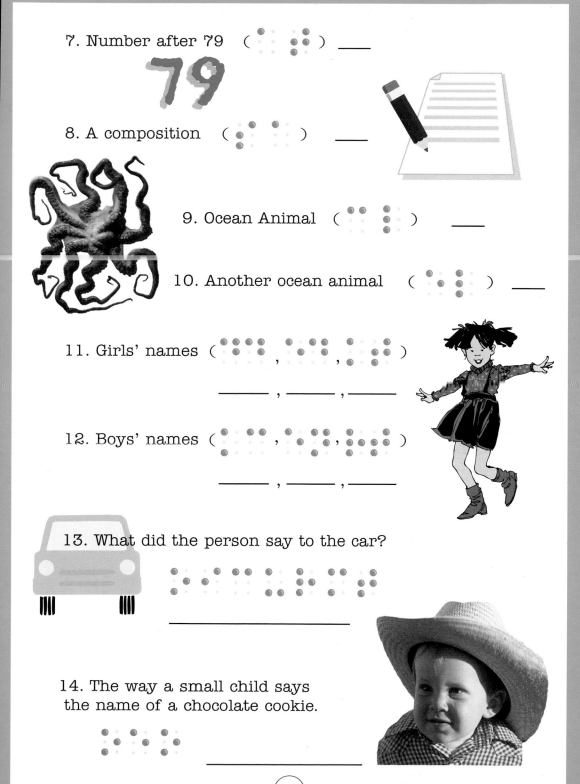

7. Number after 79   (⠀⠀⠀) ____

79

8. A composition   (⠀⠀) ____

9. Ocean Animal   (⠀⠀) ____

10. Another ocean animal   (⠀⠀) ____

11. Girls' names (⠀⠀ , ⠀⠀ , ⠀⠀)

____ , ____ , ____

12. Boys' names (⠀⠀ , ⠀⠀ , ⠀⠀)

____ , ____ , ____

13. What did the person say to the car?

_____

14. The way a small child says
the name of a chocolate cookie.

_____

13

Hidden Pictures

1.
2.
3.
4.
5.
6.
7.
8.
9.
10.
11.
12.
13.
14.
15.
16.
17.
18.
19.
20.

Matching

The three braille alphabet letters in the left column have been rearranged differently in the right column. Match the three letters in the two columns.

M J S _ J M s

Left		Right
1.		1.
2.		2.
3.		3.
4.		4.
5.		5.
6.		6.
7.		7.
8.		8.
9.		9.
10.		10.

Circle the one that does not fit with the group

Analogies

Use the blank braille cells to complete these analogies.

1.  is to as  is to

2. 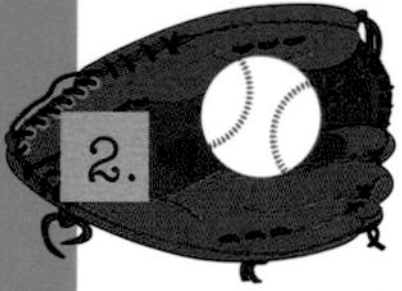 is to as  is to

3.  is to as  is to

4.  are to as  are to

5.  is to as  are to

6. 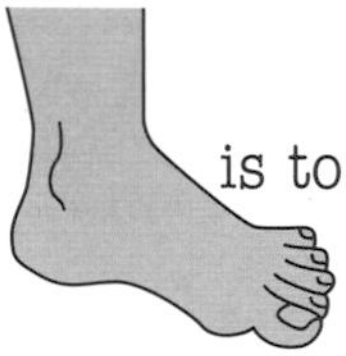 is to as 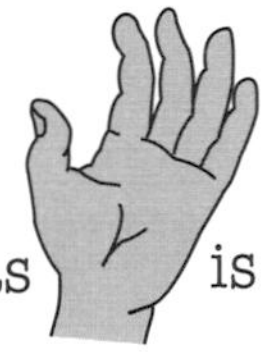 is to

7.  is to as  is to

8.  is to as  is to

9.  is to as  are to

The pictures plus the braille form what compound words?

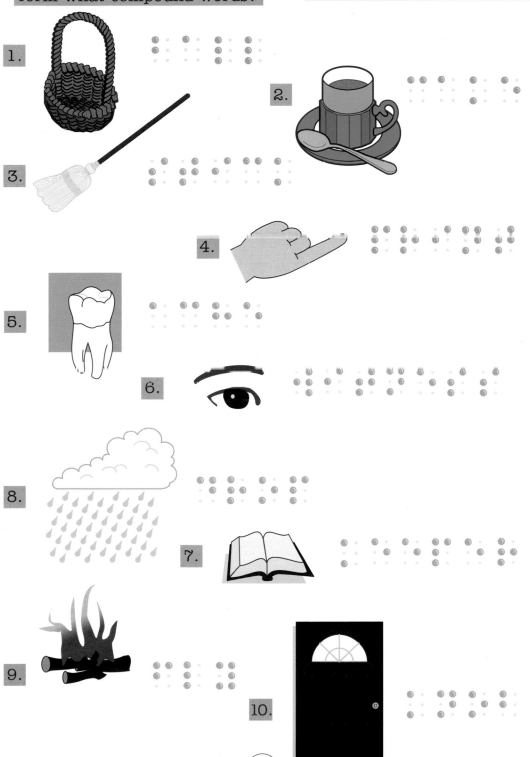

1.

2.

3.

4.

5.

6.

7.

8.

9.

10.

19

Capital Letters

You now know the lower case letters. How are capital letters distinguished? The capital sign is dot 6 in the cell immediately before the letter to be capitalized.

A lower case g ⠛ becomes a capital G like this ⠠⠛

You can now braille proper names:

Elena

Canada

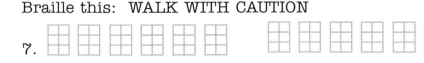

Translate these proper names:

1.

2.

3.

4.

Braille this proper name: Walt Disney

5.

Now, suppose that two dot 6s come immediately before a word. Let's use Mexico:

and the result is MEXICO

Translate these:

6.

Braille this: WALK WITH CAUTION

7.

Use your knowledge of capital and lower case letters to answer these questions:

My first name is

My last name is

I live in (place)

I have either traveled to or would like to travel to these two countries:

For me, the best holiday of the year is

but the worst holiday is

A person who inspires me is

Sounds Good to Me

Rhyming Words. Which words rhyme?

1. why

2. see

3. fix

4. shoe

5. toes

Homophones. Which words sound alike?

1.
2.
3.
4.
5.
6.

Antonyms. Braille a word that is the opposite.

1. add

2. proud

3. crooked

4. idle

5. doubt

Wordsearch

Find and circle the following celestial items. They are
spelled across, up, down, backward, and diagonally.

Mercury	Mars	Neptune	Galaxy	Sun ✓
Venus	Saturn	Uranus	Comets	Moon
Earth	Jupiter	Pluto	Star	

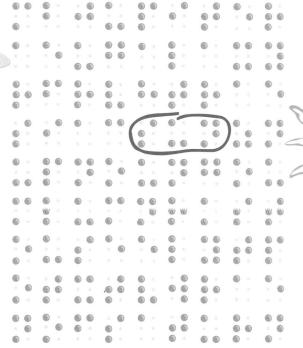

Make your own wordsearch!

Complete the grid by placing these words:

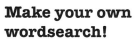

     red
     green
     purple
     blue
     pink

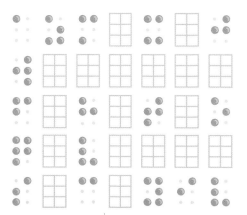

23

Crossword Puzzle

Use the clues listed below to name the sports and complete the puzzle.

DOWN

1. ball, net and racket
2. sword or foil
3. uses a wicket
4. gloves, ring and rounds

ACROSS

5. drop, header and goal
6. type of football
7. snow and slopes

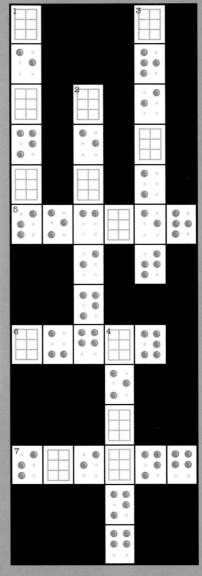

Numbers

are based on the alphabet letters A - J. To distinguish a number, this sign 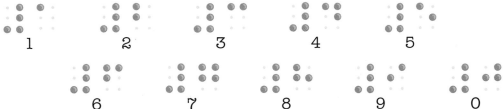 comes before the letter sign. Thus, the number sign followed by an A is the number 1. The number sign followed by B is the number 2 and so on.

1   2   3   4   5

6   7   8   9   0

Adding to 10. Each box contains one number. Draw a circle around any two neighboring numbers that add up to ten.

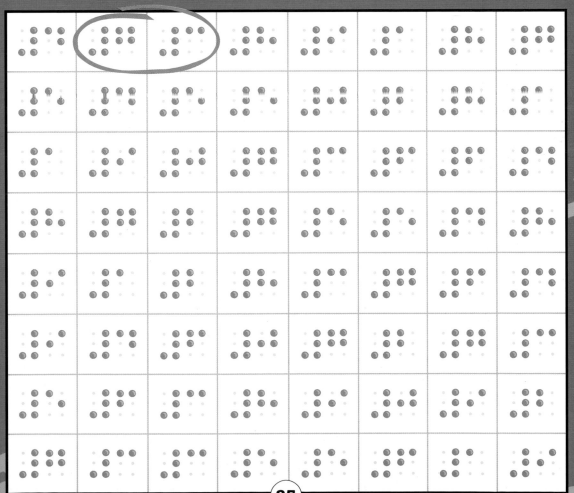

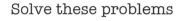

Number Practice

Solve these problems

a) $5 +$ ⚃⚃ $=$ ▦▦

b) $3 \times$ ▦▦ $=$ ⚃⚃⚃⚃

c) $10 \div$ ▦▦ $=$ ⚃⚃

d) ▦▦ $\times 6 =$ ⚃⚃⚃

e) ⚃⚃⚃⚃ $-$ ▦▦▦ $= 57$

f) $100 +$ ▦▦▦ $=$ ⚃⚃⚃⚃

g) ⚃⚃⚃⚃ $-$ ⚃⚃⚃⚃ $=$ ▦▦▦▦

h) ▦▦▦▦ $\div$ ⚃⚃⚃ $=$ ⚃⚃⚃

i) ⚃⚃ $\times$ ⚃⚃ $=$ ▦▦▦

j) $5 \times$ ⚃⚃ $+ 7 -$ ⚃⚃ $=$ ▦▦▦

Number Practice

Find these numbers on the Bingo cards. Five in a row vertically, horizontally or diagonally wins the game!

Page 6 & 7

A - J Recognition

1. bag	8. idea
2. ace	9. cage
3. jab	10. acid
4. hid	11. badge
5. fib	12. decide
6. hide	13. beaded
7. jade	14. jagged
	15. egghead

Page 8 & 9

K - T Recognition

1. pot	8. rattle
2. lost	9. image
3. fold	10. slang
4. room	11. phase
5. clock	12. orphan
6. onion	13. orange
7. knock	14. neglect
	15. sailplane

Page 10 & 11

U - Z Recognition

1. bye	8. wait
2. ivy	9. extra
3. yes	10. crazy
4. few	11. onyx
5. way	12. mixture
6. buoy	13. volume
7. buzz	14. velvet
	15. zippy

Page 12 & 13

Alphabet Answers

1. j	8. s a
2. t	9. c l
3. c	10. e l
4. i	11. dd, ed, kt
5. o	12. kc, en, rt
6. g	13. o i c u r m t
7. a t	14. o e o

Page 16

Matching

Page 17

Find the Mismatch

1. canary	5. clarinet
2. peach	6. gold
3. start	7. beach
4. car	8. ivy

Page 18

Analogies

1. waddle   (hop)

2. throw   (kick)

3. air   (water)

4. bush   (tree)

5. skin   (shell)

6. big toe   (thumb)

7. draw   (paint)

8. boy   (girl)

9. window   (eyes)

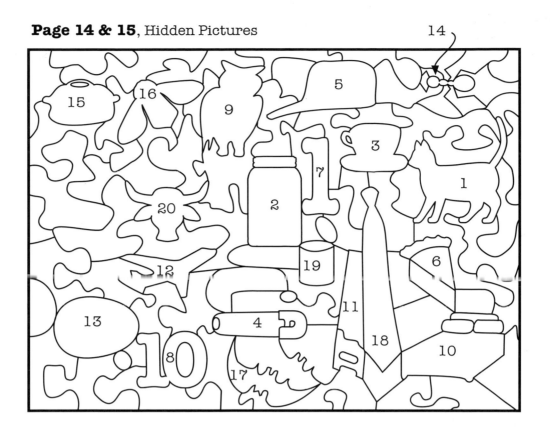

Page 19
Compound Words
1. basketball
2. cupcakc
3. broomstick
4. fingerprint
5. toothache
6. eyewitness
7. raindrop
8. bookkeeper
9. firefly
10. doorknob

Page 20
Capital Letters
1. Quebec
2. Lake Erie
3. Emily
4. Jupiter
5.

6. a FUN person

7.

Page 22
Rhyming Words
1. why ✓   pie ✓
2. see   guy
3. fix   flea
4. shoe ✓ blue ✓
5. toes ✓ nose ✓
Homophones
1. cent ✓ sent ✓
2. see   scent
3. seas ✓ seize ✓
4. right   road
5. rode   write
6. wring   red

Page 23, Wordsearch

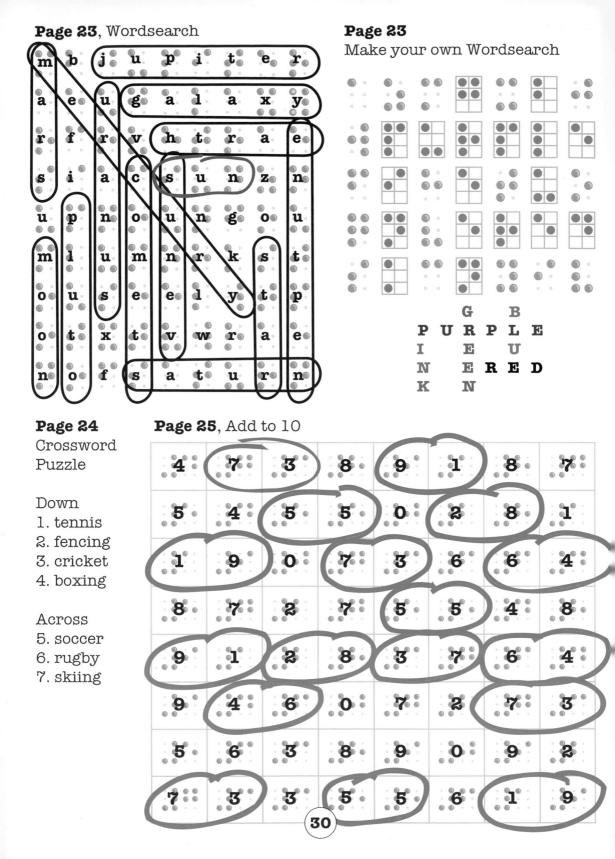

```
m  b  j  u  p  i  t  e  r
a  e  u  g  a  l  a  x  y
r  f  r  v  h  t  r  a  e
s  i  a  c  s  u  n  z  n
u  p  n  o  u  n  g  o  u
m  l  u  m  n  r  k  s  t
o  u  s  e  l  y  t  p
o  t  x  t  v  w  r  a  e
n  o  f  s  a  t  u  r  n
```

Page 23
Make your own Wordsearch

```
      G     B
P  U  R  P  L  E
I     E     U
N     E  R  E  D
K     N
```

Page 24
Crossword
Puzzle

Down
1. tennis
2. fencing
3. cricket
4. boxing

Across
5. soccer
6. rugby
7. skiing

Page 25, Add to 10

```
4  7  3  8  9  1  8  7
5  4  5  5  0  2  8  1
1  9  0  7  3  6  6  4
8  7  2  7  5  5  4  8
9  1  2  8  3  7  6  4
9  4  6  0  7  2  7  3
5  6  3  8  9  0  9  2
7  3  3  5  5  6  1  9
```

Page 26, Number Practice

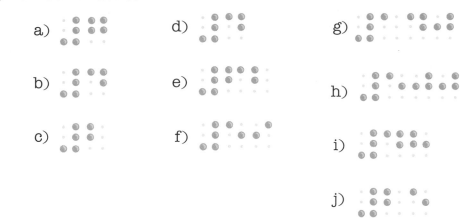

a)
b)
c)
d)
e)
f)
g)
h)
i)
j)

Page 27, Number Practice

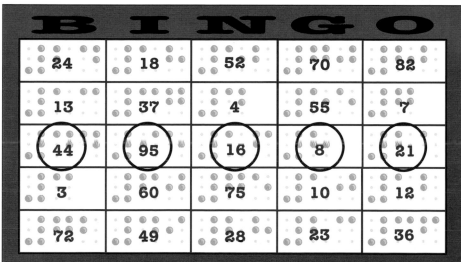

B	I	N	G	O
24	18	52	70	82
13	37	4	55	7
(44)	(95)	(16)	(8)	(21)
3	60	75	10	12
72	49	28	23	36

B	I	N	G	O
84	2	52	37	21
76	41	89	8	35
63	59	75	22	91
24	37	16	10	12
7	68	18	14	85

Also from Garlic Press

Finger Alphabet GP-046
Uses word games and activities to teach the finger alphabet.

Signing in School GP-047
Presents signs needed in a school setting.

Can I Help? Helping the Hearing Impaired in Emergency Situations GP-057
Signs, sentences and information to help communicate with the hearing impaired.

Caring for Young Children: Signing for Day Care Providers and Sitters
GP-058 Signs for feelings, directions, activities and foods, bedtime, discipline and comfort-giving.

An Alphabet of Animal Signs
GP-065 Animal illustrations and associated signs for each letter of the alphabet.

Mother Goose in Sign GP-066
Fully illustrated nursery rhymes.

Number and Letter Games
GP-072 Presents a variety of games involving the finger alphabet and sign numbers.

Expanded Songs in Sign GP-005
Eleven songs in Signed English. The easy-to-follow illustrations enable you to sign along.

Foods GP-087
A colorful collection of photos with signs for 43 common foods.

Fruits & Vegetables GP-088
Thirty-nine beautiful photos with signs.

Pets, Animals & Creatures
GP-089 Seventy-seven photos with signs of pets, animals & creatures familiar to signers of all ages.

Coyote & Bobcat GP-081
A Navajo story serving to tell how Coyote and Bobcat got their shapes.

Raven & Water Monster GP-082
This Haida story tells how Raven gained his beautiful black color and how he brought water to the earth.

Fountain of Youth GP-086
This Korean folk tale about neighbors shows the rewards of kindness and the folly of greed.

Ananse the Spider: Why Spiders Stay on the Ceiling GP-085
A West African folk tale about the boastful spider Ananse and why he now hides in dark corners.

www.garlicpress.com